D0346330

700023570524

ZERO TO TEN

Published in Great Britain in 2001 by ZERO TO TEN Limited,
327 High Street, Slough, Beikshire SL1 1TX

First Published in Australia by The Five Mile Press
12 Summit Road, Noble Park North, Victoria 3174 Australia

Copyright © 1986 The Five Mile Press

All rights reserved.
No part of this publication may be reproduced or utilized in any form or by any means,
electronic or mechanical, including photocopying, recording or by any information retrieval system,
without the prior written permission of the Publishers.

A CIP catalogue record for this book is available from the British Library.

ISBN 1-84089-132-7

Printed and bound in Singapore

Terry's Tricycle

BOB GRAHAM

WORCESTERSHIRE COUNTY COUNCIL	
052	
BfS	25 Feb 2003
J531	£ 4.50

Bill knows of a special
place to ride his tricycle.

It's not on the grass.
The grass is much too soft
and the wheels sink in.

It's not in the deep puddles,
but they are lots of fun.

It's not in the mud.
The wheels get stuck.
Look how he has to push.

He can't push the pedals
with Terry the Terror.

Bill can't go anywhere with
Terry in the back.

It's hard to push the pedals on the carpet.
The wheels sink in here, too.

It's easier to push the pedals on the
kitchen floor. Look at Terry slide.

Look at Bill slip.
It's more slippery with the water.

Here is his special place,
a hard, smooth path.
It's much easier to push
the pedals.

Look at him go!

The path is much better than
all the other places.

Easier than the grass
and the puddles.

Easier than the mud
and the carpet.

Bill can stop with the toes
of his shoes on the stones.

Background Notes for Parents and Teachers

We use Energy all the time, to push and pull, lift and carry. We can use our Energy more efficiently when we use wheels and pulleys and cogs.
Other forces, like Gravity or Friction, also affect how much Energy we use. Because Gravity pulls everything downwards, we use less Energy cycling down a hill, but more if we want to go up. If the surface is smooth, we use less Energy to move across it, but if it is rough, we use more.

Experiments to try with children

1. Place a brick on a flat, smooth surface (like the kitchen floor).
    Without jerking, push the brick along and estimate how much energy is used.

2. To investigate how gravity affects it, create a slope with a long piece of wood. Place the brick on top of the slope and push it down. Does this take more or less energy? Does the brick move more or less quickly? Then try again making the slope more and less steep.

3. To investigate how friction affects it, place the brick on different kinds of surfaces: smooth, hard tiles, a woolly carpet, grass, a gravel path.

4. Finally, try placing the brick on something which has wheels – a toy car or skateboard would do. Now push again – what can be observed?